SEEDING HEAVEN
PREPARING FOR REVIVAL
KEITH DUNCAN

HIS CALL

HIS CALL MINISTRIES, INC

HISCALL.TV

CONTENTS

HOW TO USE THIS GUIDE

This study guide is designed to help you go deeper into the message of *Seeding Heaven: Preparing for Revival.* It is ideal for both individual and group study. Each chapter includes a Scripture Focus, Key Insights with fill-in-the-blank interaction, a Summary Insight, SELAH reflection questions, and an Activation challenge.

For personal use: Take time to prayerfully work through each section, journaling your thoughts and encounters.

For group use: Read the chapter together, use the SELAH questions for discussion, and encourage each person to take the Activation step during the week.

May this guide not only deepen your understanding but also ignite hunger and action as you seed the heavens for revival.

Prayer of Invitation

Holy Spirit, open my eyes to see, open my ears to hear, and open my heart to receive. Stir my hunger and use this guide to seed revival in me. Let every truth become alive in my spirit, and let my life become fertile ground for Your glory. Amen.

CHAPTER 1
CLOUD SEEDING

Scripture Focus

"Be patient, then, brothers and sisters, until the Lord's coming. See how the farmer waits for the land to yield its valuable crop, patiently waiting for the autumn and spring rains." (James 5:7, NIV)

Key Insights (Fill-in-the-Blank)

1. Revival is not _____ — it is _____.

2. Just as scientists release particles into clouds to produce rain, believers are called to release _____, _____, and _____ into the heavens to prepare for outpouring.

3. God always _____ before He _____.

Summary Insight

Revival is not random — it is seeded. Just as scientists use cloud seeding to release rain, God calls us to "seed the heavens" with prayer, worship, fasting, and faith. This chapter reminds us that God restores before He pours. He prepares the atmosphere of our lives and churches so His Spirit can be released like rain. Seeding Heaven means positioning ourselves to be vessels of His glory.

SELAH

1. What are some practical ways you can "seed the heavens" in your personal life this week?

_____

_____

_____

2. Why is atmosphere so important when preparing for revival?

_____

_____

_____

3. How does the principle of "God restores before He pours" give you hope in your current season?

_____

_____
_____

4. What seeds are you currently sowing in prayer or worship that you believe will bring breakthrough?

_____
_____
_____

5. How can you partner with others to create a prepared atmosphere in your home, church, or city?

_____
_____
_____

Activation

Take 10 minutes today to "seed the heavens." Choose one spiritual seed — a prayer, a song, or a scripture declaration — and release it intentionally. Journal what you sense in your spirit as you do this.

(Take action this week and be ready to share your testimony.)

CHAPTER 2

THE ATMOSPHERE OF EDEN

Scripture Focus

"Surely the Lord is in this place, and I was not aware of it... This is none other than the house of God; this is the gate of heaven." (Genesis 28:16–17, NIV)

Key Insights (Fill-in-the-Blank)

1. Dr. Myles Munroe taught that everything God created was designed for a specific _____.

2. Eden was more than a garden — it was the atmosphere of God's _____.

3. When man lost Eden, he lost his _ _ _ _ _ _ _ _, and revival is God restoring us back into it.

Summary Insight

Dr. Myles Munroe often taught that everything God created was designed for a specific environment. A fish needs water, a seed needs soil, and man needs the presence of God. Eden was more than a garden — it was the atmosphere of God's presence. When man lost Eden, he lost his environment. Revival is God restoring us back into the atmosphere where His glory can dwell. When we cultivate Eden's atmosphere through worship, prayer, and obedience, we function in the fullness of our design and release the fragrance of His glory.

SELAH

1 Why did Dr. Myles Munroe emphasize environment as the key to a product's full potential?

_____
_____
_____

2. How does Jacob's encounter at Bethel illustrate the importance of atmosphere?

_____

_____
_____

3. What happens when people (or churches) function outside of the atmosphere of God's presence?

_____
_____
_____

4. What are some "toxic atmospheres" you need to remove from your life to make room for His presence?

_____
_____
_____

5. How can you intentionally cultivate an "Eden atmosphere" in your daily life?

_____
_____
_____

Activation

Identify one space (your home, office, or car) and dedicate it as your "Eden place." Fill it with worship, prayer, and scripture until it becomes an atmosphere where you sense God's nearness.

(Take action this week and be ready to share your testimony.)

CHAPTER 3

THE WAR IN THE HEAVENS NOW

Scripture Focus

"For our struggle is not against flesh and blood, but against the rulers, against the authorities, against the powers of this dark world and against the spiritual forces of evil in the heavenly realms." (Ephesians 6:12, NIV)

Key Insights (Fill-in-the-Blank)

1. The battle we face is not against _ _ _ _ _ _ and _ _ _ _ _ _, but against spiritual forces in the heavenly realms.

2. Satan's strategy has always been to block the _ _ _ _ _ _ between God and man.

3. Worship, prayer, and declaration are not optional — they are our spiritual _ _ _ _ _ _ in the war for the heavens.

Summary Insight

There is a real war taking place in the heavens. Scripture reminds us that our struggle is not against flesh and blood but against rulers, authorities, and spiritual forces of darkness. Satan's primary objective has always been to disrupt the flow between God and man. This is why cultivating an atmosphere of worship and prayer is so vital — it clears the airways for Heaven's glory to break through. Revival requires people who will contend in the Spirit, knowing their battle is not earthly but heavenly.

SELAH

1. How does Ephesians 6:12 shift your perspective about the true nature of spiritual battles?

_____

_____

_____

2. Why is it dangerous to view people as the enemy rather than spiritual forces at work?

_____

_____

_____

3. What are some ways the enemy tries to block communication between God and His people today?

_____

_____

_____

4. How can worship and prayer serve as weapons in spiritual warfare?

_____

_____

_____

5. Where do you sense God calling you to contend more intentionally in the Spirit?

_____

_____

_____

Activation

Set aside time this week to engage in intentional spiritual warfare prayer. Pray over your family, your church, and your city, declaring victory and breakthrough in the name of Jesus. Use Scripture as your weapon and worship as your battle cry.

(Take action this week and be ready to share your testimony.)

CHAPTER 4

PRAISE

THE SOUND THAT SHIFTS THE SKIES

Scripture Focus

"God inhabits the praises of His people."
(Psalm 22:3, KJV)

Key Insights (Fill-in-the-Blank)

1. Praise is not about personal preference — it is about creating an atmosphere that God _____.

2. The sound of praise disarms the enemy and releases _____ into the atmosphere.

3. True praise is not ego-centric but _____ —
focused on the King and not ourselves.

Summary Insight

Praise is the sound that shifts the skies. Scripture declares
that God inhabits the praises of His people. This means
praise creates a seat for Him to dwell. When we praise,
the atmosphere shifts and the enemy's grip is broken. The
heavenly sound of Revelation 4–5 shows us worship that
is completely centered on the King — not on human need
or preference. When we align our sound with Heaven's,
God's glory fills the room.

SELAH

1. How does Psalm 22:3 describe God's relationship to our
praise?

_____

_____

_____

2. What happens in the atmosphere when believers release
true praise?

_____

_____

_____

3. Why is it important to distinguish between ego-centric and theo-centric worship?

_____
_____
_____

4. How can studying Revelation 4–5 reshape the way we view praise?

_____
_____
_____

5. What are some practical steps you can take to make your praise more God-centered this week?

_____
_____
_____

Activation

Spend time this week praising God with songs and declarations that focus solely on Him. Lay aside requests and simply magnify His greatness until you sense the atmosphere shift. Take note of how God's presence responds to the sound of your praise.

(Take action this week and be ready to share your testimony.)

CHAPTER 5

TONGUES

HEAVEN'S LANGUAGE ON EARTH

Scripture Focus

"For anyone who speaks in a tongue does not
speak to people but to God. Indeed, no one
understands them; they utter mysteries by the
Spirit." (1 Corinthians 14:2, NIV)

Key Insights (Fill-in-the-Blank)

1. Speaking in tongues is not speaking to men but to
_____.

2. Tongues release _____ of the Spirit that the
natural mind cannot grasp.

3. Praying in tongues strengthens your _____ and builds your inner man.

Summary Insight

Tongues are Heaven's language on earth. Paul reminds us in 1 Corinthians 14:2 that the one who speaks in a tongue speaks to God, not man. This is a direct line of communication with the Father, by-passing human understanding. Tongues release mysteries, build faith, and align us with God's perfect will. When we pray in the Spirit, we are edified, strengthened, and equipped to carry revival fire.

SELAH

1. According to 1 Corinthians 14:2, who is the primary recipient when we speak in tongues?

_____
_____
_____

2. What does Paul mean when he says that tongues release 'mysteries by the Spirit'?

_____
_____
_____

3. How has praying in tongues strengthened your faith in times of weakness or uncertainty?

_____

_____

_____

4. Why is it important to edify your spirit through tongues if you desire to carry revival fire?

_____

_____

_____

5. What practical step can you take to cultivate a daily rhythm of praying in tongues?

_____

_____

_____

Activation

Set aside 15 minutes each day this week to pray in tongues. Ask the Holy Spirit to strengthen your spirit, reveal mysteries, and align your prayers with God's will. Write down any impressions, scriptures, or visions He gives you during this time.

(Take action this week and be ready to share your testimony.)

CHAPTER 6

PROPHETIC DECLARATIONS
SPEAKING TO SHIFT

Scripture Focus

"The tongue has the power of life and death, and those who love it will eat its fruit." (Proverbs 18:21, NIV)

Key Insights (Fill-in-the-Blank)

1. The tongue carries the power of _ _ _ _ _ _ and _ _ _ _ _ _.

2. Prophetic declarations align our words with God's

_ _ _ _ _ _ _ _.

3. Speaking God's Word has the authority to shift _ _ _ _ _ _ _ and release breakthrough.

Summary Insight

Our words carry weight. Proverbs 18:21 tells us the tongue has the power of life and death. Prophetic declarations are not wishful thinking — they are Spirit-inspired words that align with Heaven's decree. When we boldly declare God's promises, we shift atmospheres, tear down strongholds, and release breakthrough. Declarations remind us and the enemy that God's Word is final authority.

SELAH

1. What does Proverbs 18:21 teach us about the power of our words?

_____

_____

_____

2. How do prophetic declarations differ from casual or careless words?

_____

_____

_____

3. What are some promises from Scripture that you can begin to declare over your life and family?

_____

_____

_____

4. How have you seen words of faith shift an atmosphere or bring breakthrough in the past?

_____

_____

_____

5. Why is it important to combine declarations with listening for God's voice?

_____

_____

_____

Activation

Choose three Scriptures this week and turn them into prophetic declarations. Speak them aloud daily over your life, family, and church. Pay attention to how these declarations begin to shift your mindset and the atmosphere around you.

(Take action this week and be ready to share your testimony.)

CHAPTER 7

PROPHETIC WORSHIP
SOUNDWAVES OF GLORY

Scripture Focus

"God is spirit, and his worshipers must worship in the Spirit and in truth." (John 4:24, NIV)

Key Insights (Fill-in-the-Blank)

1. Prophetic worship is not about performance but about

_ _ _ _ _ _ _ _.

2. In prophetic worship, the setlist submits to the

_ _ _ _ _ _ _ _.

3. Worship leaders are called to be gatekeepers who release Heaven's _ _ _ _ _ _ _ _ on earth.

Summary Insight

Prophetic worship is Heaven's dialogue with earth. It is not about performance but enthronement. True worshipers release their song to the King and then wait for His response. When we discern the antiphonal flow — God responding to our worship with His word — Heaven kisses earth, and His glory is revealed. Prophetic worship requires space, sensitivity, and boldness to release the new sound of Heaven.

SELAH

1. What does John 4:24 teach us about the posture of true worship?

_____

_____

_____

2. How is prophetic worship different from simply singing songs on a setlist?

_____

_____

_____

3. Why is it vital for worship leaders to act as gatekeepers rather than performers?

_____

_____

_____

4. What does it mean to discern the 'antiphonal flow' in worship?

_____

_____

_____

5. How can you cultivate greater sensitivity to the Spirit's leading during worship?

_____

_____

_____

Activation

During your next time of worship, pause between songs and listen for the Spirit's response. Release what you sense — whether it's a spontaneous song, a scripture, or a declaration. Allow God's voice to shape the atmosphere.

(Take action this week and be ready to share your testimony.)

CHAPTER 8

PROPHETIC INTERCESSION

BIRTHING REVIVAL IN PRAYER

Scripture Focus

"And I sought for a man among them who should build up the wall and stand in the breach before me for the land, that I should not destroy it, but I found none." (Ezekiel 22:30, ESV)

Key Insights (Fill-in-the-Blank)

1. Prophetic intercession is standing in the _ _ _ _ _ _ _ _ for others and for nations.

2. Intercession is more than prayer requests — it is partnering with God to _____ His purposes.

3. Revival is birthed when God's people cry out with _____ and persistence.

Summary Insight

Prophetic intercession is the act of standing in the gap. It is prayer fueled by the Spirit, crying out for Heaven's will to manifest on earth. Ezekiel 22:30 reveals God's longing for someone to intercede, to hold back judgment, and to call forth mercy. Intercession is not passive — it is priestly work that births revival. Through fasting, travail, and persistent prayer, prophetic intercessors become midwives of awakening.

SELAH

1. What does it mean to 'stand in the gap' according to Ezekiel 22:30?

_____

_____

_____

2. How is prophetic intercession different from simply presenting prayer requests?

_____

_____

_____

3. Why is persistence so important in intercession?

_____

_____

_____

4. Have you ever sensed a burden from the Lord to intercede for someone or something? What happened?

_____

_____

_____

5. How can intercessory prayer prepare the way for revival in your church or city?

_____

_____

_____

Activation

Ask the Holy Spirit to place a burden of intercession on your heart this week. Commit to pray daily for that person, situation, or nation. Record what you sense God speaking and how He answers through your prayers.

(Take action this week and be ready to share your testimony.)

CHAPTER 9

THE NEW SOUND OF REVIVAL

Scripture Focus

"Sing to the LORD a new song; sing to the LORD, all the earth." (Psalm 96:1, NIV)

Key Insights (Fill-in-the-Blank)

1. Every move of God throughout history has carried a unique _____.

2. The 'new sound' is not man-made creativity but Spirit-_____ expression that carries God's presence.

3. When the authentic sound of Heaven is released, it produces transformation that no _____ can counterfeit.

Summary Insight

The new sound of revival is not about creative novelty — it is about Heaven's breath on worship. History shows us that each outpouring of the Spirit brought with it a sound: hymns during the Great Awakenings, scripture songs in the Charismatic Renewal, and prophetic worship in more recent movements. But the 'new sound' God desires is Spirit-breathed, carrying His weight and presence. It is a sound that cannot be manufactured or imitated — when released, it produces transformation that impacts congregations, cities, and nations.

SELAH

1. What does Psalm 96:1 mean when it calls us to 'sing a new song'?

_____

_____

_____

2. How has God used different sounds in past revivals to shift atmospheres?

_____

----

3. Why is it dangerous to pursue creativity for creativity's sake instead of Spirit-breathed worship?

----

4. What is the difference between the counterfeit 'sound' of the world and the authentic sound of Heaven?

----

5. How can you personally position yourself to release Heaven's sound in worship?

Activation

Take time this week to wait on the Lord during worship. Ask Him to release a new song in your spirit — whether a melody, a phrase, or a declaration. Sing or speak it out boldly, trusting that His Spirit will breathe life on it.

(Take action this week and be ready to share your testimony.)

CHAPTER 10

HOSTING HIS PRESENCE

Scripture Focus

"The LORD replied, 'My Presence will go with you, and I will give you rest.'" (Exodus 33:14, NIV)

Key Insights (Fill-in-the-Blank)

1. Hosting the presence of God is not a duty but an _____.

2. God's presence is not ornamental but _____ — it establishes His rule and releases transformation.

3. When we host Him well, He entrusts us with fresh
_____ and assignments.

Summary Insight

Hosting God's presence is both a privilege and a responsibility. Exodus 33 reminds us that His presence is what sets us apart from all other people. Hosting Him requires sensitivity, honor, and alignment with His purposes. It is not about goosebumps or emotional moments, but about creating a resting place for His glory. When we host Him well, His presence commissions us, releases fresh assignments, and transforms entire regions.

SELAH

1. What does Exodus 33:14 reveal about the value of God's presence?

_____

_____

_____

2. Why is hosting God's presence described as an opportunity rather than a burden?

_____

_____

_____

3. What is the difference between ornamental presence and governmental presence?

_____

_____

_____

4. How can a church or community cultivate an atmosphere where God is honored to stay?

_____

_____

_____

5. What fresh assignments might God release when His presence is truly hosted?

_____

_____

_____

Activation

Dedicate intentional time this week to simply host God's presence. Create space for Him in worship and prayer without agenda, and ask Him to show you how to honor His presence in new ways. Write down what He reveals to you.

(Take action this week and be ready to share your testimony.)

CHAPTER 11

CARRIERS OF THE GLORY

Scripture Focus

"For the earth will be filled with the knowledge of the glory of the LORD as the waters cover the sea." (Habakkuk 2:14, NIV)

Key Insights (Fill-in-the-Blank)

1. Revival fire is _ _ _ _ _ _ _ _ — it spreads from one carrier of glory to another.

2. To carry the glory, we must be willing to be _ _ _ _ _ _ _ _ by His presence.

3. God is raising up carriers who will release His glory into
_ _ _ _ _ _ _ _, cities, and nations.

Summary Insight

Revival fire is contagious. Every person who encounters the glory of God is called to carry it and release it. Randy Clark's impartation at Toronto spread to Steve Hill at Brownsville and beyond, showing how one spark can ignite a movement. Michele and I have often said we were ruined by His presence — once you taste His glory, you cannot go back to ordinary church. Carriers of the glory are those who burn with His fire and release it wherever they go, ushering in transformation.

SELAH

1. What does Habakkuk 2:14 reveal about God's ultimate plan for His glory?

_____

_____

_____

2. How does revival history show that glory is carried from one person or place to another?

_____

_____

_____

3. What does it mean to be 'ruined by His presence'?

_____

_____

_____

4. Where have you personally experienced God's glory in a way that marked you forever?

_____

_____

_____

5. How can you become a carrier of His glory in your home, church, and community?

_____

_____

_____

Activation

Ask God this week to make you a carrier of His glory. Spend time in His presence until you sense His fire stirring in you, then look for opportunities to release what He has placed in you. Pray for someone, declare His word, or simply share your testimony — and watch the fire spread.

(Take action this week and be ready to share your testimony.)

CHAPTER 12
BUILD FOR ME A PLACE

Scripture Focus

"Thus says the LORD: 'Heaven is my throne, and the earth is my footstool. Where is the house that you will build for me? And where is the place of my rest?'" (Isaiah 66:1, NKJV)

Key Insights (Fill-in-the-Blank)

1. God is not looking for programs — He is looking for a
_ _ _ _ _ _ _ _.

2. Revival culture is built when God's people create a place of sustained _ _ _ _ _ _ _ _.

3. To build Him a place, we must be Spirit-led, Passion-driven, and _ _ _ _ _ _ _ _-focused.

Summary Insight

The ultimate call of revival is habitation. God asks in Isaiah 66:1, 'Where is the house you will build for me?' He is not after events, but dwelling places. Building Him a place means creating altars in our homes, churches, and communities where His glory can rest. This requires tearing down consumer Christianity and pursuing His presence above all else. When we build Him a place, He fills it with His glory and releases transformation that impacts generations.

SELAH

1. What does Isaiah 66:1 teach us about God's desire for a dwelling place?

_____
_____
_____

2. Why is sustained presence more important than momentary visitation?

_____
_____
_____

3. How can we build revival cultures rather than just host revival events?

_____
_____
_____

4. What idols or distractions must be torn down in order to truly make room for God's glory?

_____
_____
_____

5. Where is God calling you personally to 'build Him a place' — in your home, church, or city?

_____
_____
_____

Activation

This week, take intentional steps to 'build Him a place.' Set aside a room in your home, gather others for worship, or begin establishing rhythms of prayer and fasting. Ask the Lord to make you a dwelling place for His glory and write down the ways He confirms His presence.

(Take action this week and be ready to share your testimony.)

PRAYER OF IMPARTATION & COMMISSIONING

Father, I thank You for every seed of truth planted through these pages. I ask that You would seal everything I have read and studied, that it would not be stolen or forgotten, but watered by Your Spirit and bear fruit in due season.

Use me to seed the heavens for revival in my home, my church, my city, and the nations. I yield myself as a carrier of Your glory. Let my life be an altar where Your fire never goes out. In Jesus' Name, Amen.

Antiphonal Response: "Yes, I agree and receive it in Jesus' Name!"

www.ingramcontent.com/pod-product-compliance
Lightning Source LLC
Chambersburg PA
CBHW070650130626
46555CB00006B/2809